12 IMMIGRANTS WHO MADE
AMERICAN
TECHNOLOGY GREAT

by Tristan Poehlmann

12 STORY LIBRARY

www.12StoryLibrary.com

12-Story Library is an imprint of Bookstaves.

Photographs ©: Library of Congress, cover, 1; Library of Congress, 4; Associated Press, 5; Deborah Dobson-Brown/PD, 5; Library of Congress, 6; Popular Science/PD, 7; Employee(s) of MGM/PD, 8; US Patent Office/PD, 9; Priest, L C (Lt)/PD, 9; PD, 10; Mass Communication Specialist 2nd Class Chantel M. Clayton/US Navy, 11; Associated Press, 12; Evan-Amos/PD, 13; karaage831/CC2.0, 14; Mile Atanasov/Shutterstock.com, 15; Pradeep Gaur/Mint via Getty Images, 16; iunewind/Shutterstock.com, 17; NASA, 18; NASA, 19; Sossina Haile/Caltech, 20; Sakurambo/PD, 21; Demers6/CC4.0, 22; SpaceX/CC0, 23; J.Dorfman/MIT/Splash/Newscom, 24; White House/PD, 25; Steve Jurvetson/CC2.0, 26; Twinsterphoto/Shutterstock.com, 27; Vintage Tone/Shutterstock.com, 27; PD, 28; Stanford School of Engineering, 29

ISBN
978-1-63235-578-2 (hardcover)
978-1-63235-632-1 (paperback)
978-1-63235-693-2 (ebook)

Library of Congress Control Number: 2018937977

Printed in the United States of America
Mankato, MN
July 2018

About the Cover
Dr. Maria Telkes in 1956.

Access free, up-to-date content on this topic plus a full digital version of this book. Scan the QR code on page 31 or use your school's login at 12StoryLibrary.com.

Table of Contents

Charles Steinmetz Sparks the Electrical Industry

A brilliant engineer was almost turned away at Ellis Island. Immigration officers tried to reject him because he was disabled. They did not believe he could be a genius.

Charles Steinmetz was born in 1865 in Poland. In school, Steinmetz studied math, chemistry, and electrical engineering. He was active in socialist politics. The government of Poland did not trust socialists. In 1889, Steinmetz emigrated to escape arrest for his activism.

Due to his disability, Steinmetz stood just four feet tall. He had a hump on his back and trouble walking. Immigration officers judged him by his looks. Steinmetz had to convince them that he was intelligent. Finally he was allowed to enter the United States.

In New York City, Steinmetz worked as an electrical engineer. He developed a math equation that changed his industry. Engineers designing electrical systems had trouble with magnetism. Magnetism was part of electrical systems. But it caused some loss of power. Steinmetz's math equation helped engineers figure out how much

Steinmetz in his laboratory with Thomas Edison in 1931.

power was lost. It helped them reduce the amount of power lost.

Steinmetz's math equation made long-distance power lines possible. He also invented many devices. His work helped the electrical industry grow. The US power grid was built with his ideas.

THE MARK OF A GENIUS

Steinmetz was once asked to fix a machine at a Ford factory. For two days, he listened to the machine. He did math in a notebook. Then he marked an X on the side of the machine. He told the Ford engineers to open the machine at that spot and replace the part inside. It worked. Steinmetz charged Ford $10,000: $1 for making the mark and $9,999 for knowing where to make it.

200+
Number of US patents held by Charles Steinmetz.

- Steinmetz emigrated from Poland to escape political punishment.
- He was an electrical engineer who invented many devices.
- He developed a math equation that changed electrical engineering.

Mária Telkes Captures the Sun's Energy

She was known as the Sun Queen. Mária Telkes was a physicist and an innovator. She changed how people use solar power.

Telkes was born in 1900. Her family lived in a big city in Hungary. In high school,

Telkes became interested in solar power. She decided to study physical chemistry. She learned to use physics to solve chemical problems. In 1924, Telkes earned her graduate degree. The next year, she immigrated to the United States.

While visiting a cousin in Cleveland, Telkes was offered a job. She decided to stay in the United States. She became a researcher. Later she worked for the Massachusetts Institute of Technology (MIT). Telkes studied solar energy. She invented many solar-powered devices.

In 1948, Telkes designed the first house heated entirely by solar energy. She developed an efficient heating system. It worked by storing heat in a type of salt. The salt absorbed the sun's heat. On cold days, bins of salt between the walls kept the house warm. Telkes solved a big problem. She figured out how to store solar energy.

10

Number of cloudy days in a row that Mária Telkes's solar house could remain heated.

- Telkes emigrated from Hungary in 1925 for a job.
- She was a physicist who studied solar energy.
- She invented the first solar-powered heating system.

SAVING LIVES WITH SOLAR

During World War II, the US Navy asked for Telkes's help. They needed a portable device to turn salt water into fresh water. Telkes developed a solar-powered system. The device made ocean water safe to drink. It became part of emergency medical kits. Telkes's invention saved sailors' lives.

Telkes' solar home design was featured in *Popular Science* in 1949.

Telkes continued to invent solar technology. Her work became the foundation of the solar industry. In 2012, she was added to the National Inventors Hall of Fame.

Hedy Lamarr Advances Wireless Communication

Hedy Lamarr was a famous Hollywood star. But she was also an inventor. She invented a system that changed how we communicate today.

Lamarr was born in 1914 in Austria. Her nickname Hedy was short for Hedwig. Her family was Jewish. Her father was interested in technology. He taught her how streetcars and power plants worked. Lamarr became an actor, but she liked inventions.

At eighteen, Lamarr got married. Her husband sold weapons to many countries. Lamarr learned about weapons technology. In 1937, she left her husband. The next year, she immigrated to the United States. A Hollywood movie producer had offered her a contract. Lamarr became a movie star. She invented devices as a hobby.

By 1940, World War II had taken over Europe. A German torpedo sank a ship full of refugees. It was a tragedy. Lamarr wanted to help. She thought she could make American torpedoes better. She knew about weapons technology. Torpedoes were guided by radio. An enemy could block the radio channel. But what if the channel kept changing? Lamarr invented a way to guide torpedoes that could not be blocked.

At the time, the US Navy did not understand Lamarr's idea. It took 20 years before they used her invention. But Lamarr's work changed wireless communication. It is used today for cell phones and Wi-Fi. Lamarr was added to the National Inventors Hall of Fame in 2014.

Lamarr's patent under her married name at the time, Hedy Kiesler Markey.

88
Number of radio channels Hedy Lamarr's torpedo guidance system could change between.

- Lamarr emigrated from Austria in 1938 for a job.
- She was an inventor who developed new radio technology.
- Her invention changed wireless communication.

THINK ABOUT IT

Lamarr invented her system to help win World War II. Later it was used for other purposes. How do world politics affect the development of technology?

Giuliana Tesoro Invents Flame-Resistant Fabric

was Jewish. Italy's government discriminated against Jews. It was illegal for them to go to college. Tesoro wanted to study science. In 1939, she immigrated to the United States.

Tesoro went to school at Yale University. She studied organic chemistry. At 21, she earned the highest degree in chemistry. Tesoro became a researcher. She

120+

Number of US patents held by Giuliana Tesoro.

- Tesoro emigrated from Italy to escape discrimination.
- She was a chemist who studied chemicals for use in fabric.
- She invented flame-resistant fabric.

Technology includes materials like fabric. Giuliana Tesoro was a chemist who studied fabric. Her work changed the clothes we wear.

Tesoro was born in 1921 in Italy. She grew up in the island city of Venice. Her family

REFUGEES IN WORLD WAR II

In 1939, World War II began in Europe. Jewish people were targets of violence. Many fled. Refugees came to the United States. Some were scientists, like Tesoro. These refugees brought knowledge with them. Their skills made American technology grow. Technology helped the United States become powerful. Jewish refugees changed US technology.

researched chemicals for use in fabric. Fabric can be treated with chemicals. Treated fabrics often perform better. Tesoro invented many chemical treatments. One of her inventions reduced clothes' static cling.

In 1972, Tesoro became a professor. She taught at Massachusetts Institute of Technology (MIT). She continued her research. Tesoro developed an important safety innovation. She invented flame-resistant fabric. She treated fabric with the chemical phosphorus. This made the fabric less likely to burn.

Tesoro was an expert on the technology of fabric treatments. Her work changed the safety and comfort of everyday clothing.

Ralph Baer Builds the First Video Game Console

Video game technology is always changing. Gaming has advanced since the 1960s. That's when Ralph Baer invented the first home gaming system.

Baer was born in 1922 in Germany. His family was Jewish. When Baer was eleven, he was kicked out of school. The government sent Jewish children to a separate school. Baer's family worried. Discrimination and violence were rising. In 1938, they became refugees. They immigrated to the United States.

As a teenager, Baer liked technology. He was interested in electronics. He trained to be an engineer. He could build and repair televisions. In the 1950s, Baer came up with an idea. He wanted to design a television with built-in games. But the company he worked for was not interested. His idea had to wait.

EARLY GAMING

Today many video games are like virtual reality. But the games on Baer's system were simple. They used white shapes on a dark screen. Shapes could move up and down or left to right. They could not jump or spin. Most games were based on sports. Ping-pong, golf, and target shooting were common. Games did not have stories or characters.

$100

Price in 1972 of Ralph Baer's Odyssey video game console.

- Baer emigrated from Germany with his family to escape discrimination.
- He was an electrical engineer who worked with television.
- He invented the first video gaming console.

In 1966, Baer designed the first video game console. He built the game box. It could play several games on a television. The games used simple white dots. The dots could move across the screen. Game controllers used switches and dials. Baer called the console the Odyssey. It went on sale in 1972.

Baer's work changed technology. It led to the creation of the video game industry. In 2006, Baer won the National Medal of Technology.

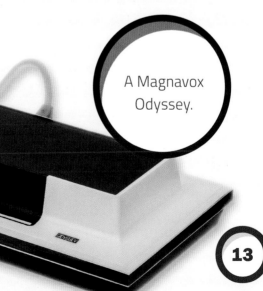

A Magnavox Odyssey.

Shuji Nakamura Lights Up LED Technology

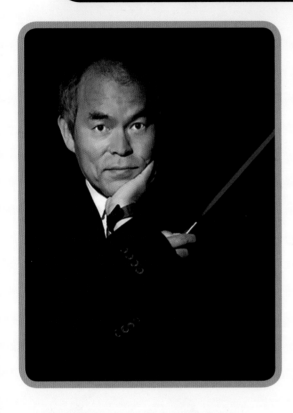

in Japan. He liked to spend time outdoors. Nature made him interested in science. In college, Nakamura studied electrical engineering. He began working as a researcher. His job was to develop new technology. But his company was small. They did not have much money for research. Nakamura became frustrated.

Light-emitting diodes (LEDs) had always interested Nakamura. The technology of light was changing. LEDs would make many products more efficient. Red LEDs existed. Nakamura wanted to develop a blue LED. Blue light would be more useful. In 1989, his company finally approved the project.

The light bulb was an amazing invention. But inventions can always be improved. Shuji Nakamura is an engineer who developed a better lightbulb.

Nakamura was born in 1954. His family lived on an island

Nakamura began his research. By 1993, he had invented a blue LED. But he kept working. He invented green and white LEDs. Efficient white light was a very important invention.

Cell phone screens are lit by Nakamura's white LEDs.

In 1999, Nakamura immigrated to the United States. He became a professor at the University of California, Santa Barbara. His work has launched a new electrical technology. In 2014, he won the Nobel Prize in Physics.

WHAT MAKES LEDS BETTER?

LED lightbulbs turn electricity into light. Other kinds of lightbulbs can do this. But they are not as efficient. Older lightbulbs turn electricity into heat. The heat makes wires inside the bulb give off light. But creating heat uses lots of electricity. LEDs do not create heat—only light. They are safer and use less electricity.

100+
Number of patents held by Shuji Nakamura.

- Nakamura emigrated from Japan in 1999 for a job.
- He is an electrical engineer who researches light technology.
- He invented blue, green, and white LEDs.

Ajay Bhatt Connects Computers with the USB

Computers connect people to information. But how do computers connect to other devices? Ajay Bhatt invented a plug that changed computer technology.

Bhatt was born in 1957 in India. His family was interested in the arts. His father was a professor. Bhatt liked sports and electronics. He taught himself how to fix clocks and radios. He could take them apart and put them back together. But he wanted to learn more about

technology. After college, he decided to go to graduate school. In 1981, he immigrated to the United States.

In New York City, Bhatt studied engineering. After graduating, he became a computer architect. He worked for Intel. His job was to develop new computer technology. In 1990, computers were not very user-friendly. Even connecting a printer to a computer was difficult. Every device used a different connector. Bhatt wanted to change that. He had

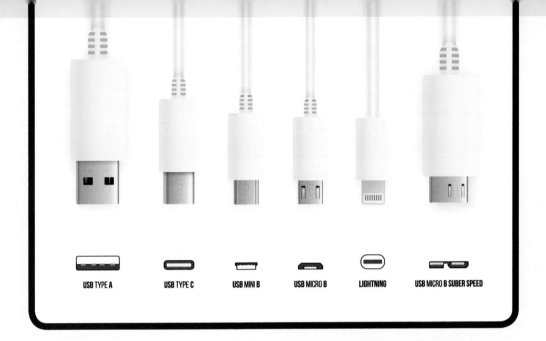

| USB TYPE A | USB TYPE C | USB MINI B | USB MICRO B | LIGHTNING | USB MICRO B SUBER SPEED |

an idea. He would develop a way to connect any device to any computer.

Bhatt based his design on a wall socket plug. He wanted a connector

that people would understand how to use. He wanted to make computers less confusing. But it took several years of work. Lots of companies had to agree to use the same connector. In 1998, the Universal Serial Bus (USB) became the standard connector. It lets any device connect to any computer.

Bhatt's invention changed technology. His work helped make computers user-friendly. Today the USB connects all kinds of products. Keyboards, phones, and data storage all plug into the same spot. Bhatt has won many awards for his invention.

Kalpana Chawla Flies into Astronaut History

loved it. Flying became her dream. She studied aircraft engineering. She was the first girl at her school to do so. But Chawla wanted to go further. In 1982, she immigrated to the United States.

Chawla went to school in Texas and Colorado. She earned the highest degree in aerospace engineering. In 1988, she joined NASA. Chawla worked on aircraft design. She helped develop the ability for aircraft to take off and land vertically. But she really wanted to be an astronaut. In 1994, she was chosen for training. Astronaut training lasted for one year.

Few people ever fly into space. Kalpana Chawla was an engineer who became an astronaut. She designed and flew in space shuttles.

Chawla was born in 1962. Her family lived in northern India. Chawla was always adventurous. When she was young, she flew in a small propeller plane. She

In 1997, Chawla flew into space. She was a crew member on the space shuttle *Columbia*. Her job was to operate the shuttle's robotic arm. The mission was to study how being weightless affects humans. The space shuttle orbited Earth 252 times.

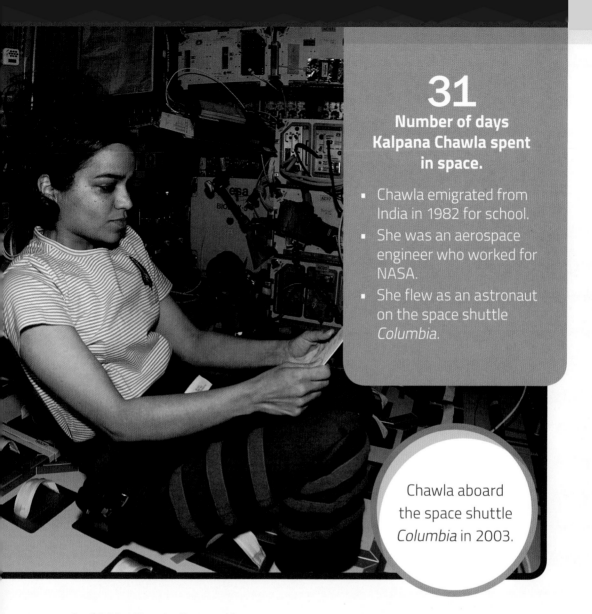

31
Number of days Kalpana Chawla spent in space.

- Chawla emigrated from India in 1982 for school.
- She was an aerospace engineer who worked for NASA.
- She flew as an astronaut on the space shuttle *Columbia*.

Chawla aboard the space shuttle *Columbia* in 2003.

In 2003, Chawla flew again on *Columbia*. The crew's mission was to conduct experiments. During takeoff, part of the shuttle's wing was damaged. Chawla's research in space went well. But when *Columbia* returned to Earth, there was a disaster. The wing damage caused the shuttle to shake apart. All the crew members died.

Chawla's work helped develop the technology of space flight. After her death, she was awarded the Congressional Space Medal of Honor.

Sossina Haile Powers the Future with Chemicals

Energy powers our world. In the future, energy will be an important resource. Sossina Haile creates new power sources for the future.

Haile was born in 1966. Her family lived in a big city in Ethiopia. Her father was a professor. When Haile was nine, Ethiopia's army took over the government. There was a violent struggle. Haile's father was almost killed. Their family fled. They became refugees. In the mid-1970s, they immigrated to the United States.

Haile's family settled in Minnesota. In school, she learned science and technology. She was the only girl in those classes. It was lonely. But she loved learning. In college, Haile studied chemical engineering. She went to Massachusetts Institute of Technology (MIT). She also studied in California and Germany. In 1992, she earned the highest degree in engineering.

Haile became a professor. She did research in a laboratory. She researched how to use chemical reactions to create energy. She wanted to make a power source like a battery. But it would last longer and produce more power. In the

2010

Year Sossina Haile won the Chemical Pioneer Award from the American Institute of Chemists.

- Haile emigrated from Ethiopia to escape violence.
- She is an engineer who studies chemical reactions.
- She invented a new technology to generate electric power.

THINK ABOUT IT

Chemical reactions produce energy that can be used to power machines. What might be the advantages of producing energy this way? What might be the disadvantages?

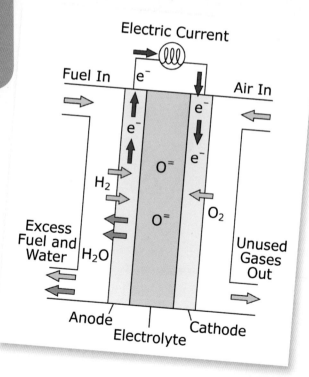

late 1990s, Haile did it. She invented a new kind of fuel cell. Fuel cells turn chemical energy into electricity. Haile's fuel cell is more efficient and less expensive. In the future, it could power an electric car.

Today, Haile is developing new ways to store solar energy. Her work helps our society prepare for the future.

Elon Musk Launches a New Space Age

Many people dream of traveling through space. Elon Musk believes that can be reality. He is working to make it possible.

Musk was born in 1971. His family lived in South Africa. Growing up, Musk loved technology. When he was 12, he created a video game. Then he sold it to a computer magazine. He was smart about business. But South Africa had a system of racial discrimination. Musk did not want to start a business there. His mother was Canadian. Musk decided to go to college in Canada. Then in 1992, he immigrated to the United States.

At the University of Pennsylvania, Musk studied physics and economics. After college, he moved to California. He planned to go to graduate school at Stanford University. But instead he joined the growing internet business. He was very successful. In 2000, he started an online payment system called PayPal. The business became popular quickly. Musk became a millionaire.

In 2002, Musk started a new business. He called it SpaceX. This was short for Space Exploration Technologies. Musk wanted to develop rockets. He believed that in the future, humans would live in space. His goal was to build a city on Mars someday. In 2008, SpaceX's *Falcon 1* rocket was launched. It orbited Earth successfully. NASA was impressed with Musk's work.

Today Musk is developing his third rocket. The *Falcon Heavy* was test launched in early 2018. Musk's work is building the space technology of the future.

20 billion
Value in US dollars of Elon Musk's rocket company SpaceX, as of 2018.

- Musk emigrated from South Africa in 1988 for school.
- He is an inventor and technology business owner.
- His work focuses on the internet and space exploration.

Dina Katabi Makes X-Ray Vision a Reality

Wireless internet (Wi-Fi) makes communication easier. But Dina Katabi discovered that it can do more than that.

Katabi was born in 1971 in Syria. She grew up in a big city. Her father and her aunts were doctors. Katabi planned to become a doctor. But she liked math

more than medicine. So she earned a degree in engineering. In 1996, she immigrated to the United States.

Katabi went to Massachusetts Institute of Technology (MIT). She studied computer science. She developed a better way to manage Internet traffic. Her work impressed MIT. They hired her as a professor. She continued making the Internet better. By 2011, she tripled the amount of traffic Wi-Fi could manage.

The next year, Katabi began a new project. She studied whether Wi-Fi could "see" through walls. Her experiments showed it was possible. Wi-Fi signals can detect movement through solid objects. By 2015, Katabi developed a way to turn the signal into an image. The image looks similar to a radar screen. It shows the shape and movement of an object. Katabi invented a type of X-ray vision.

Katabi has won a MacArthur "Genius Grant" for her work. She is developing Wi-Fi technology to make lives better.

SEEING THROUGH WALLS

Katabi's X-ray vision is a work in progress. Today it can see a person through a wall. It can tell who the person is by shape. It can track the person's movement. It can even track breathing and heart rate. Katabi developed a health monitor using the technology. But someday it could be used for entertainment, like video games.

95.7

Percent accuracy of Dina Katabi's X-ray vision at telling people apart.

- Katabi emigrated from Syria in 1996 for school.
- She is an electrical engineer and computer scientist.
- She invented a type of X-ray vision using Wi-Fi.

12

Sergey Brin Codes the Google Search Engine

The internet holds a vast amount of information. But it can be hard to find correct information. Sergey Brin made searching the internet more trustworthy.

Brin was born in 1973 in Russia. His parents were mathematicians. Their family was Jewish. Russia was not a good place for Jews. They were discriminated against. When Brin was six, his father decided they had to leave. In 1979, the family immigrated to the United States.

Brin's family moved to Maryland. His father became a professor. His mother worked for NASA. Brin learned English. He learned he was good at math. He finished high school in three years. In college, he studied math and computer science. Then he started graduate school at Stanford.

In 1995, Brin met Larry Page. They were both interested in the internet. Page had a project. He wanted to rank websites by how important they were. He thought a site's popularity could help decide its rank. He needed to find the sites that were linked to most often. Brin created an algorithm that could do that. He developed a new way to search internet sites. Brin's search engine

THINK ABOUT IT

Brin's search engine ranked sites based on how popular they were. What kinds of problems might this solve? What kinds of problems might this create?

gave users a list of sites ranked by importance. It was a huge step forward for internet users.

In 1998, Brin and Page launched a public search engine. They called it Google, for the number googol. Googol is 1 followed by 100 zeroes. Brin's work allows people to easily find information across the internet.

2.3 million
Number of searches per minute on Sergey Brin's search engine, as of 2016.

- Brin emigrated from Russia to escape discrimination.
- He is a computer scientist who founded Google.
- He and a friend created Google's search engine.

More Immigrants in History

Alexander Graham Bell

The telephone was invented by a Scottish immigrant. Alexander Graham Bell was born in 1847. He came to the United States in 1871 to teach deaf students. In 1876, he patented the telephone. Bell made the world's first telephone call to his assistant.

Qian Xuesen

NASA's Jet Propulsion Laboratory was co-founded by a Chinese immigrant. Qian Xuesen was born in 1911. In 1935, he came to the United States. He designed rocket technology. But Qian was accused of being a communist. In 1955, he was deported.

Irmgard Flügge-Lotz

For a long time, women engineering professors were rare. Irmgard Flügge-Lotz was the first at Stanford University. She was born in 1903 in Germany. In 1948, she immigrated to the United States. She became a professor of aeronautical engineering in 1961.

Vladimir Zworykin

Developing television took a while for Vladimir Zworykin. He was born in Russia 1889. In 1919, he immigrated to the United States. Over 20 years, the engineer worked on cathode ray tube (CRT) television. Television was first broadcast in 1939.

A monument honoring Vladimir Zworykin in Moscow, Russia.

Editor's note:
America is a nation of immigrants. This series celebrates important contributions immigrants have made to technology. In choosing the people to feature in this book, the author and 12-Story Library editors considered diversity of all kinds and the significance and stature of the work.

Glossary

aerospace
Earth's atmosphere and the space beyond.

algorithm
A set of steps to follow to solve a math problem or complete a computer process.

console
An electronic system that connects to a screen. Mostly used to play video games.

chemical reaction
A change that happens when two different chemicals combine.

discriminate
To unfairly treat a person or a group differently than others.

efficient
Able to work well or with little waste.

engineer
A person who designs or builds engines, machines, or systems.

fuel cell
A device that uses chemicals to produce electric power.

innovate
To do or make something in a new way.

light-emitting diode (LED)
A small device that lights up when electricity passes through it.

refugee
A person who has left their country to escape danger.

Universal Serial Bus (USB)
A special plug and cord system that connects a computer to another device.

For More Information

Books

Fraser, Mary Ann. *Alexander Graham Bell Answers the Call*. Watertown, MA: Charlesbridge, 2017.

Gibson, Karen Bush. *Women in Space: 23 Stories of First Flights, Scientific Missions, and Gravity-Breaking Adventures*. Chicago: Chicago Review Press, 2014.

Vance, Ashlee. *Elon Musk and the Quest for a Fantastic Future*. New York: HarperCollins, 2017.

Visit 12StoryLibrary.com

Scan the code or use your school's login at **12StoryLibrary.com** for recent updates about this topic and a full digital version of this book. Enjoy free access to:

- Digital ebook
- Breaking news updates
- Live content feeds
- Videos, interactive maps, and graphics
- Additional web resources

Note to educators: Visit 12StoryLibrary.com/register to sign up for free premium website access. Enjoy live content plus a full digital version of every 12-Story Library book you own for every student at your school.

Index

About the Author

Tristan Poehlmann is a freelance writer of educational nonfiction. He holds a master's degree in writing for children and young adults from Vermont College of Fine Arts. He lives in the San Francisco Bay Area.